eels
beautiful freak

Project Managers: Jeannette DeLisa and Aaron Stang
Front and Back Cover Photography by: Ann Giordano
Art Direction and Design by: Francesca Restrepo
Transcribed by: Bill LaFleur
Book Layout: Ken Rehm

© 1997 WARNER BROS. PUBLICATIONS
All Rights Reserved

Any duplication, adaptation or arrangement of the compositions
contained in this collection requires the written consent of the Publisher.
No part of this book may be photocopied or reproduced in any way without permission.
Unauthorized uses are an infringement of the U.S. Copyright Act and are punishable by law.

contents

beautiful freak . . . 3

flower . . . 42

guest list . . . 37

manchild . . . 61

mental . . . 46

my beloved monster . . . 34

not ready yet . . . 23

novocaine for the soul . . . 8

rags to rags . . . 18

spunky . . . 52

susan's house . . . 14

your lucky day in hell . . . 56

beautiful freak

Words and Music by
E

Gtr. 1 uses
Dropped D tunning:
⑥ = D

Slowly ♩. = 44

*Keyboard arr. for guitar.

hold throughout

Verse 1:

1. You're such a beau-ti-ful freak. I wish there were more just like you. You're not like all of the oth-ers. And

Beautiful Freak - 5 - 1
PG9662

© 1996 ALMO MUSIC CORP. and SEXY GRANDPA MUSIC (ASCAP)
All Rights Administered by ALMO MUSIC CORP.
on behalf of SEXY GRANDPA MUSIC for the World
All Rights Reserved

Chorus:
Eb Bb/D Eb/C Bb Eb Bb/D Eb/C Bb
that is why I love you, beau - ti - ful freak, beau - ti - ful freak.
Rhy. Fig. 2
Gr. 1
8va
T A B
Rhy. Fig. 2A
*Gtr. 2
8va
mp hold throughout
T A B
*Piano arr. for guitar.
Eb Bb/D Eb/C Bb Eb Bb/D Eb/C Bb
That is why I love you, beau - ti - ful freak, beau - ti - ful freak.
8va
end Rhy. Fig. 2
T A B
(8va)
end Rhy. Fig. 2A
T A B

Dm G Dm G Dm G Dm G
Rhy. Fig. 3
end Rhy. Fig. 3
Rhy. Fig. 3A
(8va)
end Rhy. Fig. 3A
Verses 2 & 3:
w/Rhy. Fig. 1 (Gtr. 1) simile
Dm G F C Dm G F C
2. Some peo - ple think you have a prob - lem, but that prob - lem lies on - ly with them..
3. See additional lyrics
Gtr. 2
(8va)
Dm G F C
Just 'cause you are not like the oth - ers. 2. But
Chorus 2 & 3:
w/Rhy. Figs. 2 (Gtr. 1) & 2A (Gtr. 2)
E♭ B♭/D E♭/C B♭
that is why I love you,
3. See additional lyrics
(8va)

E♭ B♭/D E♭/C B♭ E♭ B♭/D
beau - ti - ful freak, beau - ti - ful freak. That is why
E♭/C B♭ E♭ B♭/D E♭/C B♭
To Coda
I love you, beau - ti - ful freak, beau - ti - ful freak.
Bridge:
A♭ E♭/G E♭ B♭/D A♭ E♭/G E♭ B♭/D
Too good for this world, but I hope you will stay.
8va
T A B
A♭ E♭/G D♭ Cm7
And I'll be here to see that you don't fade a - way.
(8va)

Verse 3:
You're such a beautiful freak,
I bet you are flying inside.
Dart down and then go for cover.

Chorus 3:
And know that I, I love you,
Beautiful freak, beautiful freak.
You know that I, I love you,
Beautiful freak, beautiful freak.

novocaine for the soul

Words and Music by
E and MARK GOLDENBERG

Moderately ♩ = 86

Intro:
Gtr. 1   N.C.
Rhy. Fig. 1

*Play 3 times
end Rhy. Fig. 1*

Verse 1:
w/Rhy. Fig. 1 (Gtr. 1) 2 times

1. Life is hard and so am I. You better give me something so I don't die.

Chorus:
C#   F#m   C#   F#m   B   F#

No- vo- caine for the soul be- fore I sput- ter out.

Gtr. 1
mf hold throughout

C#   B   F#   C#   N.C.

Be- fore I sput- ter out.

Novocaine for the Soul - 6 - 1
PG9662

© 1996 ALMO MUSIC CORP. and SEXY GRANDPA MUSIC (ASCAP),
LONGITUDE MUSIC CO. and FAUX MUSIC (BMI)
All Rights on behalf of SEXY GRANDPA MUSIC Administered by ALMO MUSIC CORP. for the World
All Rights Reserved

Verse 2:
C♯ F♯m C♯ F♯m C♯ F♯m
Life is white and I am black. Je-sus and his law-yer
Rhy. Fig. 1
C♯ F♯m
Chorus:
C♯ F♯m C♯ F♯m
are com-ing back. Oh, my dar-ling, will you be here
end Rhy. Fig. 1
B F♯ C♯ B F♯
be-fore I sput-ter out? Be-fore I sput-ter out.
C♯ B F♯ N.C.
Be-fore I sput-ter out.

Bridge:

Guess who's liv-ing here with the great un-dead.

This paint by num-bers life is fuck-ing with my head, once a-gain.

Novocaine for the Soul - 6 - 3
PG9662

Guitar Solo:
w/Rhy. Fig. 1 (Gtr. 1)
C♯ F♯m C♯ F♯m C♯ F♯m
*Gtr. 2
mf hold bend
hold bend
Gtr. 3
*w/tremolo and delay.
Verse 3:
w/Rhy. Fig. 1 (Gtr. 1)
C♯ F♯m C♯ F♯m C♯ F♯m
Life is good
and I feel great
Gtr. 2 out
trem. bar
hold
Gtr. 3 out
C♯ F♯m C♯ F♯m
'cause moth-er says I was
a great mis-take.
Chorus:
C♯ F♯m
No - vo - caine
C♯ F♯m C♯ F♯m C♯ F♯m
for the soul.
You bet-ter give me some-thing
to fill the hole

be - fore I sput - ter out.   Be - fore I sput - ter out.

Be - fore I sput - ter out.

end Rhy. Fig. 2

Novocaine for the Soul - 6 - 5
PG9662

B F♯ C
Outro:
B F♯
Be- fore I sput - ter out.
Gtr. 1
Gtr. 4
C♯ B F♯ C♯
1/2
B F♯ C♯ B F♯ C♯
rit.
rit.

susan's house

Words and Music by
E and JIM JACOBSEN
(and JIM WEATHERLY)

Freely
Intro:
N.C.
3 sec. synth. effects

Moderately ♩ = 84
Bass figure

Verses 1, 2 & 3:
Cont. bass fig. simile

1. (Spoken:) Going over to Susan's house, walking south down Baxter Street,
2. 3. See additional lyrics

*Gtr. 1
Rhy. Fig. 1

*Synthesizer arr. for guitar (tacet first four measures on Verse 3 only).

nothing hiding behind this picket fence. There's a crazy old woman smashing

end Rhy. Fig. 1

Susan's House - 4 - 1
PG9662

© 1996 ALMO MUSIC CORP. (ASCAP), WB MUSIC CORP. (ASCAP), CALLIPYGIAN MUSIC (ASCAP),
SEXY GRANDPA MUSIC (ASCAP) and POLYGRAM INTERNATIONAL PUBLISHING INC. (ASCAP)
All Rights on behalf of CALLIPYGIAN MUSIC Administered by WB MUSIC CORP.
All Rights Reserved
*Contains samples from "LOVE FINDS IT'S OWN WAY" (By JIM WEATHERLY),
POLYGRAM INTERNATIONAL PUBLISHING, INC. (ASCAP)

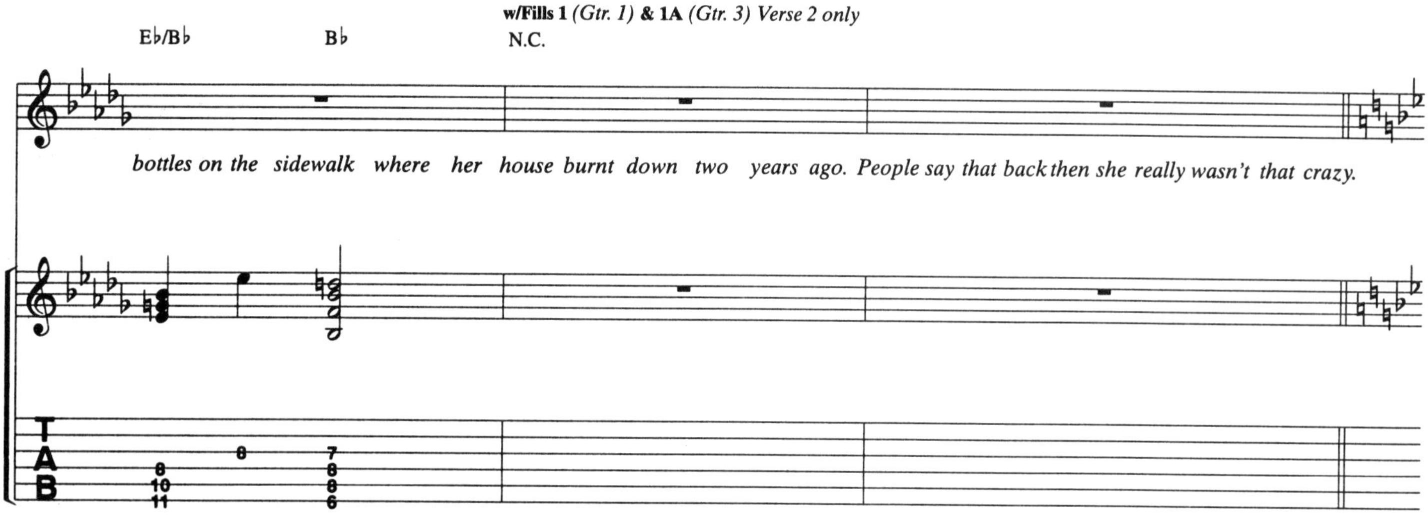
w/Fills 1 (Gtr. 1) & 1A (Gtr. 3) Verse 2 only
E♭/B♭
B♭
N.C.
bottles on the sidewalk where her house burnt down two years ago. People say that back then she really wasn't that crazy.

Chorus:
B♭
E♭
Cm7
E♭/F
Go - ing o - ver to Su - san's house.
*Gtr. 2
Rhy. Fig. 2
*Elec. piano arr. for fingerstyle guitar.

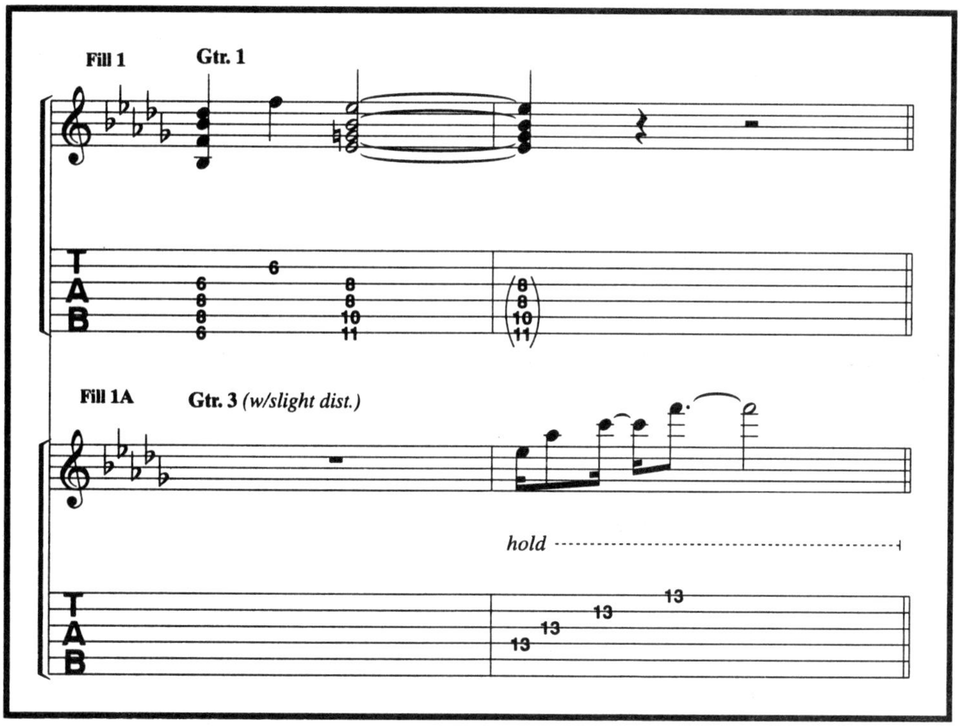
Fill 1
Gtr. 1
Fill 1A
Gtr. 3 (w/slight dist.)
hold

Going over to Su - san's house, I can't be a - lone to - night.

__ gon - na make it right.

Bridge:

Take a left down Ech - o Park, a kid asks do I want some crack?

T V sets are spew - ing Bay - wach through the win - dows in - to black.

D.S. 𝄋 al Coda

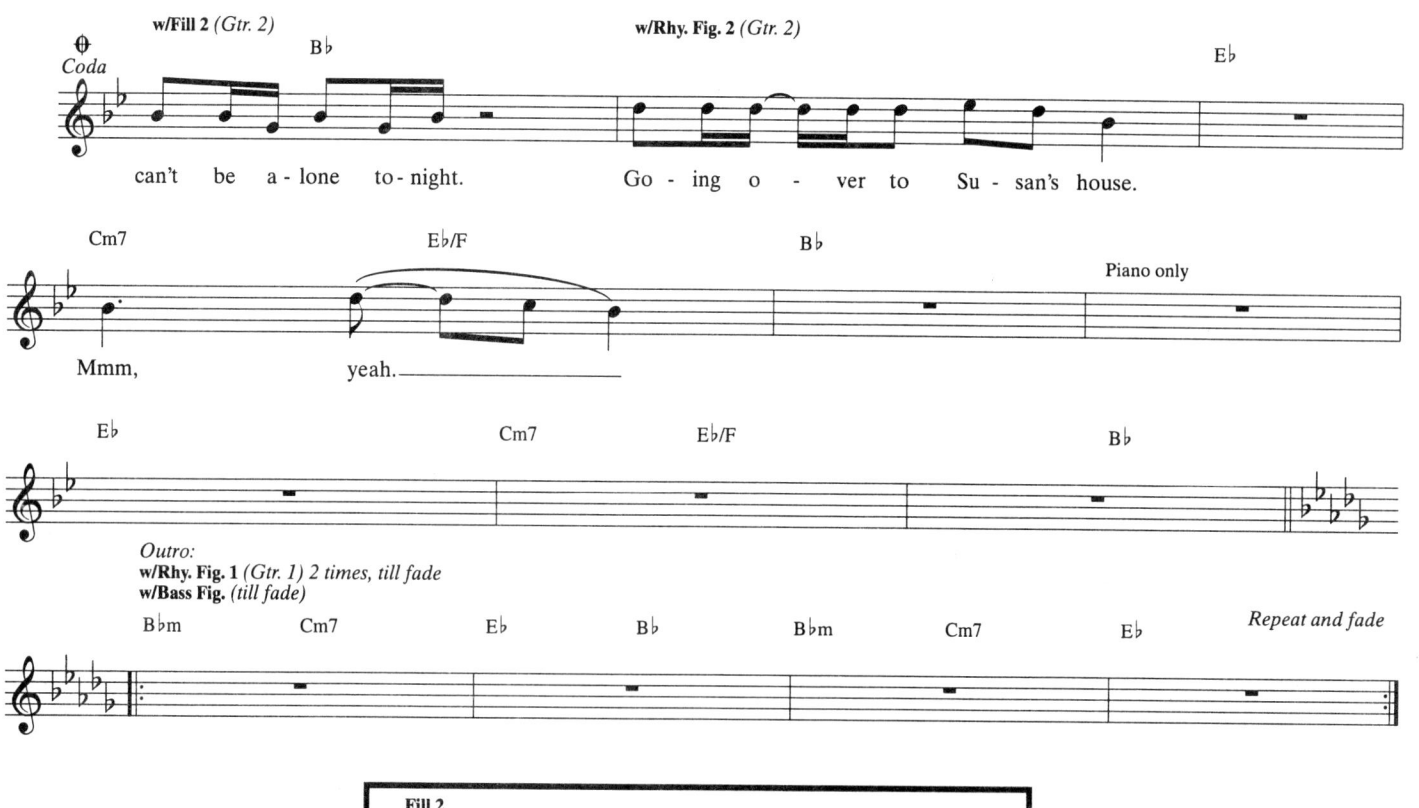

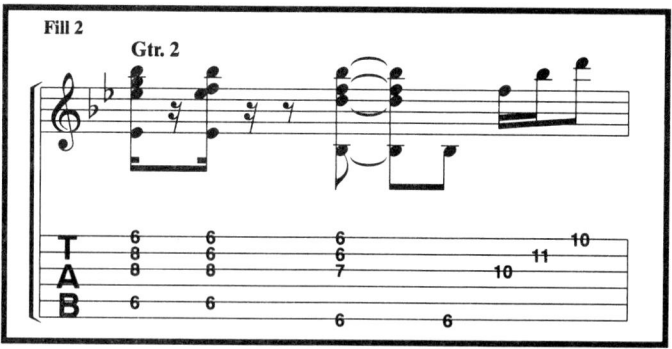

Verse 2:
(Spoken:) Down by the Doughnut Prince, a fifteen year old boy lies on the sidewalk with a bullet in his forehead.
In a final act of indignity, the paramedics take off all his clothes for the whole world to see while they put him in the bag.
Meanwhile, an old couple argues inside the Queen Bee, the sick fluorescent light shimmering on their skin.
(To Chorus:)

Verse 3:
(Spoken:) Here comes a girl with long brown hair who can't be more than seventeen.
She sucks on a red popsickle while she pushes a baby girl in a pink carriage.
And I'm thinking, "That must be her sister, that must be her sister, right?"
They go into the Seven-Eleven and I keep walking, and I keep walking.
(To Chorus:)

rags to rags

Words and Music by
E

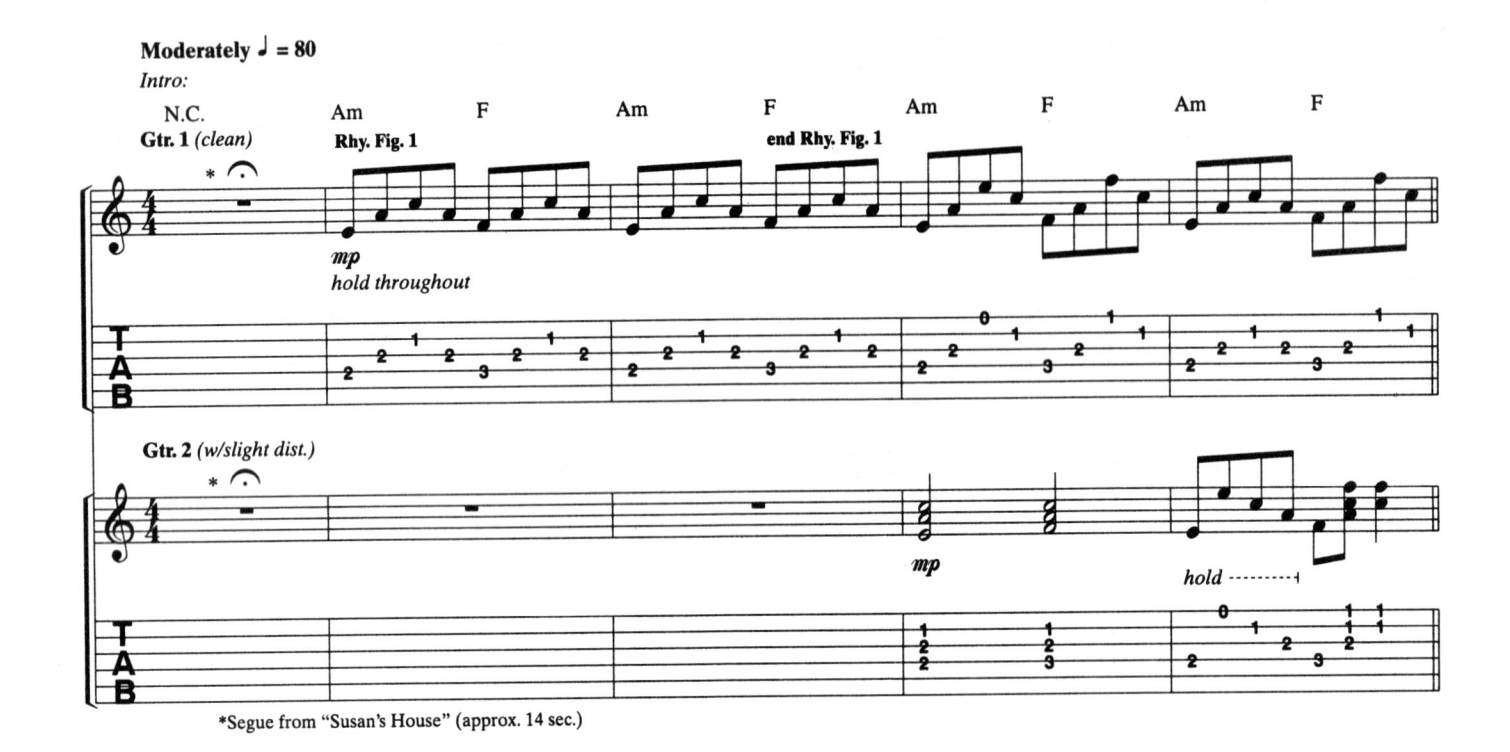

Moderately ♩ = 80

*Segue from "Susan's House" (approx. 14 sec.)

Verse 1:
1. There's a spi-der crawl-ing on the bath-room mir-ror, right on top of my right eye.

Rags to Rags - 5 - 1
PG9662

© 1996 ALMO MUSIC CORP. and SEXY GRANDPA MUSIC (ASCAP)
All Rights Administered by ALMO MUSIC CORP. on behalf of SEXY GRANDPA MUSIC for the World
All Rights Reserved

w/Rhy. Fig. 1 (Gtr. 1) 1½ times
Am F Am F Am F
And I can't stop star - ing back. How did I get this way? Take a big look at a liv - ing
Gtr. 2
hold hold hold hold hold hold
Chorus:
G C F C G C
lie. Rags to rags and rust to rust.
Gtrs. 1 & 2
Rhy. Fig. 3
end Rhy. Fig. 3
mf
w/dist.
F C G C F C
How do you stand when you've been crushed?
G C B♭ F Am F Am F
w/Rhy. Fig. 1 (Gtr. 1)
So rags to rich - es was a bust.

20

Verse 2:

Rags to Rags - 5 - 4

Verse 3:
D.S. 𝄋 al Coda
Am F Am F Am F
3. And one day I'll come through my A-mer-i-can dream. But it won't mean a fuck-ing thing.
Gtr. 1
Gtr. 2
hold
Coda
w/Rhy. Fig. 3 (Gtrs. 1 & 2) 4 times
G C F C
So rags to rags and rust to rust. Don't let me go.
Rags to rags and rust to rust. Don't let me go.
Rags to rags and rust to rust. Don't let me go.
w/Rhy. Fig. 3 (Gtrs. 1 & 2)
Repeat and fade

not ready yet

Words and Music by
E and JON BRION

Verse 1:
Em Bm G Em Bm G
world out - side. And I know 'cause I've heard talk. In my
Gtr. 1
mp w/clean tone
hold throughout
Em Bm G Em Bm G
sweet - est dream I would go out for a walk. But I
Chorus:
Em Bm G Em Bm G
don't think I'm read - y yet. I'm not feel - ing up to it now.
Gtr. 1
Rhy. Fig. 2
Gtr. 2
Rhy. Fig. 2A

Em Bm G Em Bm G
Just not that stead - y yet. And I don't need you tell - ing me how. 2. There's some
end Rhy. Fig. 2
end Rhy. Fig. 2A
Verse 2:
Em Bm G Em Bm
hap - pi - ness, and my stone face cracks a - gain.
mf w/dist.
mf w/dist.

26

Chorus:
w/Rhy. Figs. 2 (Gtr. 1) & 2A (Gtr. 2) simile

Maybe sometime sooner or later. But I don't think I'm ready yet. I'm not feeling up to it now. Just not that steady yet. And I don't need you telling me how.

Not Ready Yet - 11 - 4
PG9662

Guitar Solo:
G
Em
Bm
G
Gtr. 1
Rhy. Fig. 3
mf w/dist.
Gtr. 2
mf w/dist.
Gtr. 3
mf w/dist.
Em
Bm
G
end Rhy. Fig. 3
Em
Bm
hold
hold
hold
hold

G
Em
Bm
G
3. So if I
Gtr. 3 out
hold
hold
hold
Verse 3:
Em
Bm
G
Em
Bm
leave my room,— don't you tell— me to light - en up.
Gtr. 1
w/clean tone
mp
Gtr. 2
TAB

D.S. 𝄋 al Coda
G
Em
Bm
G
May - be some - time soon - er or lat - er. But I
mp w/clean tone
T
A
B

Coda
G
Em
Bm
G
I don't need you tell - ing me how. I
Gtr. 1
Gtr. 2
T
A
B

w/Rhy. Fig. 3 (Gtr. 1) simile
Em Bm G Em Bm
don't need you tell - ing me how.
Don't need you tell - ing me how.
mf w/dist.
mf w/dist.
G Em Bm G
I don't need you tell - ing me how.
Gtr. 2
Gtr. 3

31

Outro:
w/Rhy. Fig. 3 *(Gtr. 1)* 2½ times, simile

Dont need you tell - ing me__ how.__

Not Ready Yet - 11 - 9
PG9662

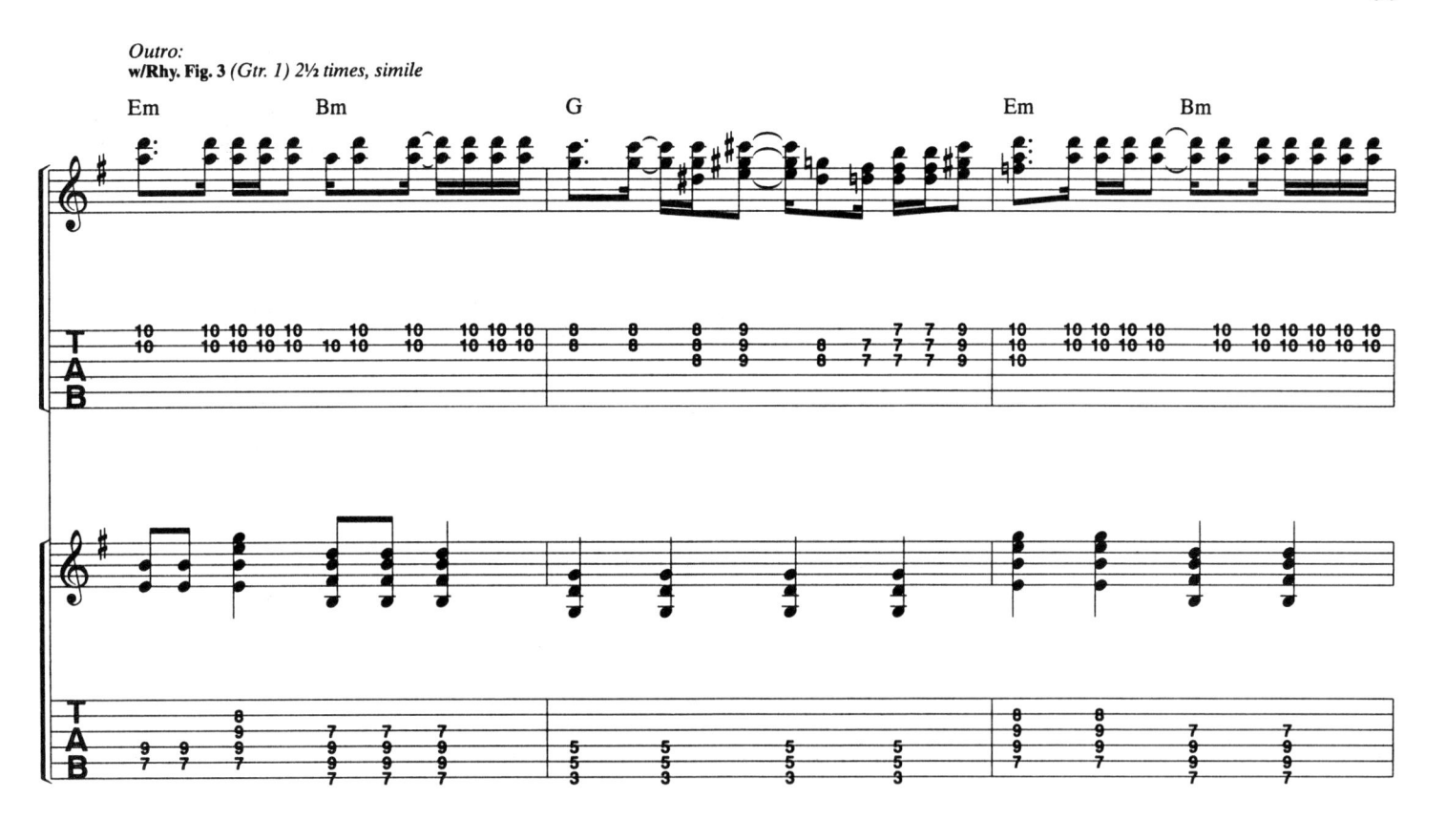

32

Don't need you tell-ing me how. Don't, don't need you tell-ing me how.

Not Ready Yet - 11 - 10
PG9662

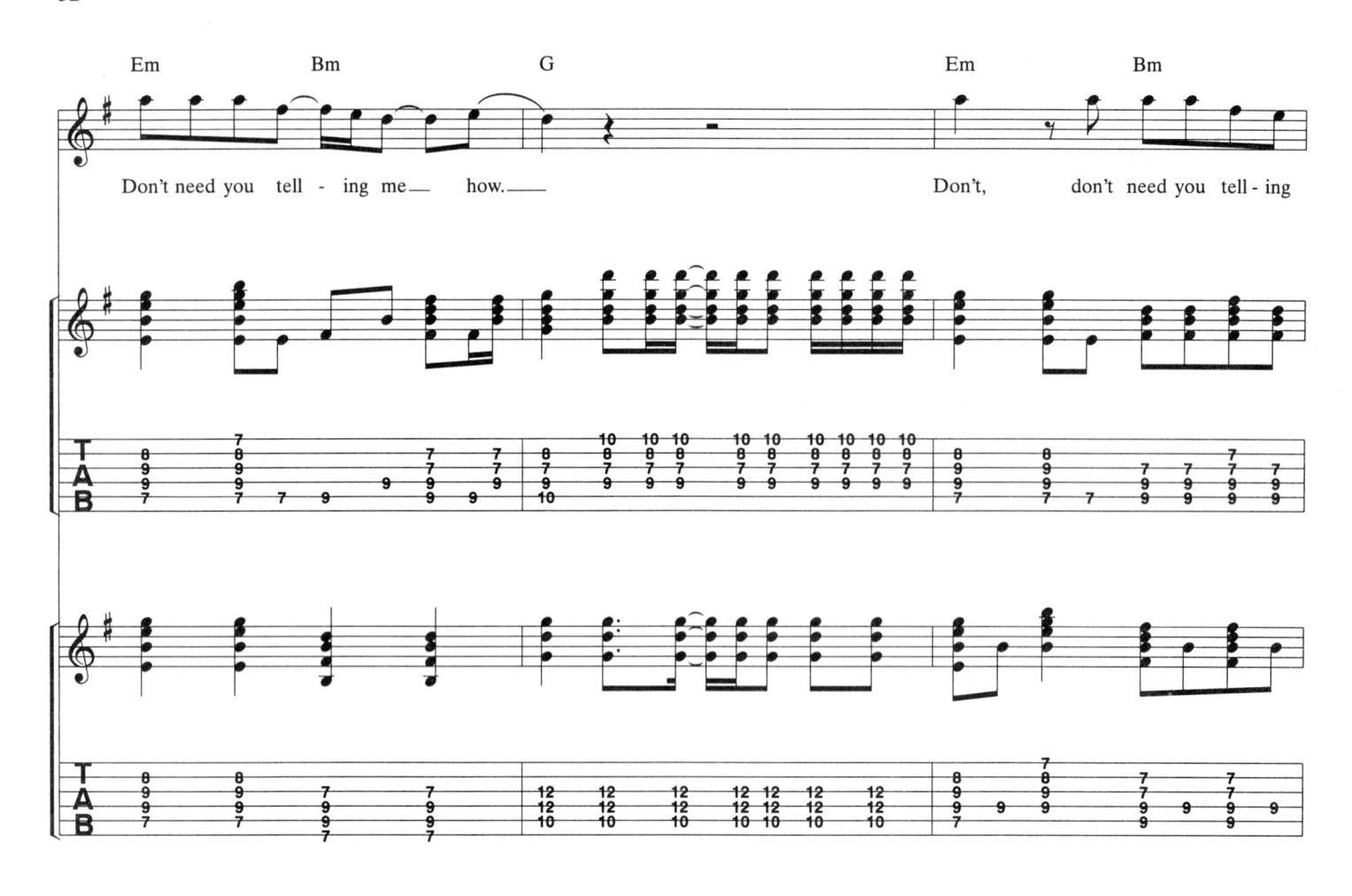

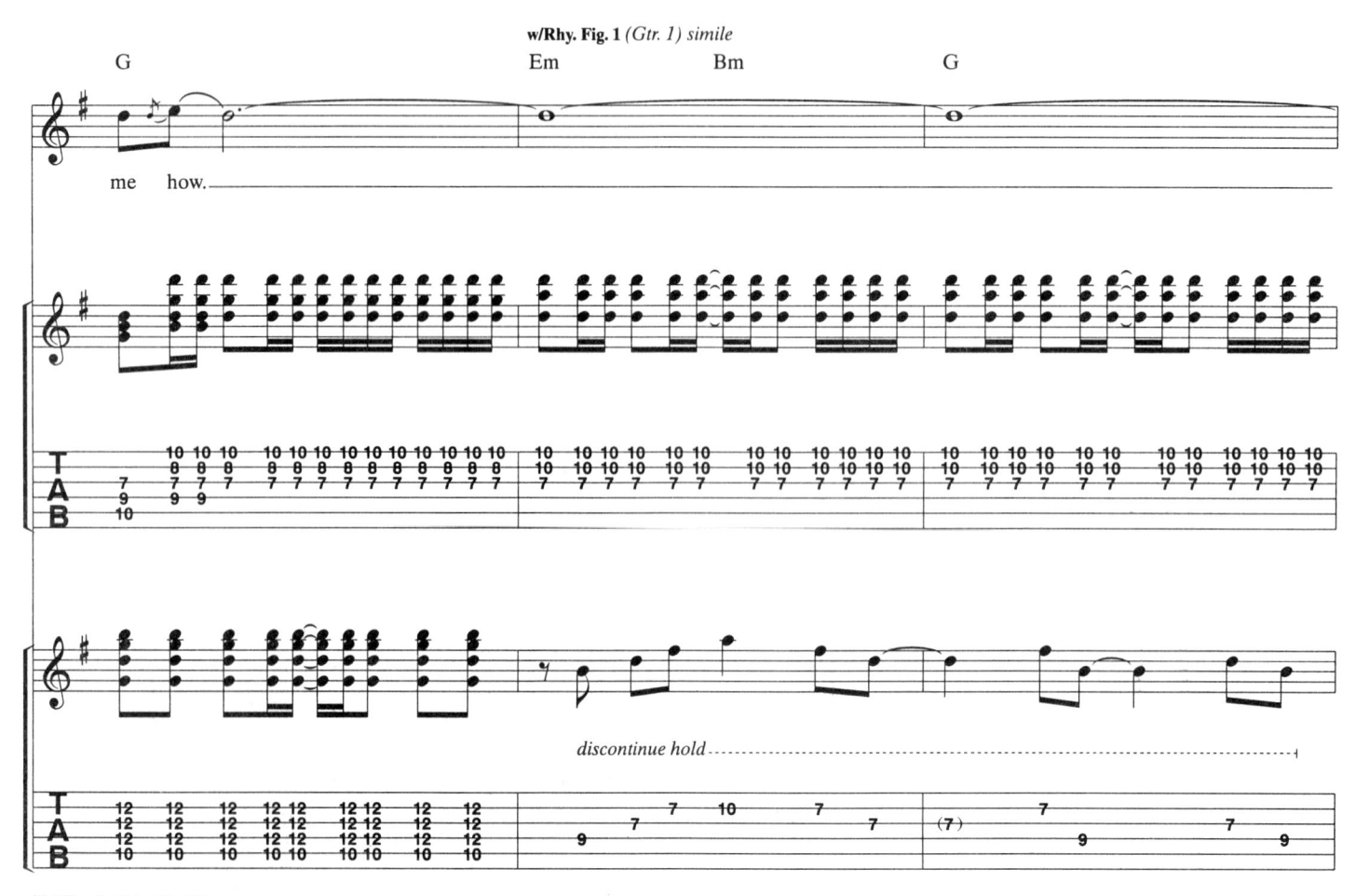

33

*Harmonic analysis derived from all parts combined.

Not Ready Yet - 11 - 11
PG9662

… # my beloved monster

Words and Music by
E

Moderately ♩ = 98

Intro:
N.C. Banjo — Rhy. Fig. 1 Gtr. 1 — A D A D — end Rhy. Fig. 1
mf w/slight dist.

Verses 1 & 2:
w/Rhy. Fig. 1 (Gtr. 1) 4 times

1. My be-lov-ed mon-ster and me, we go ev-'ry-where to-geth-er.
2. *See additional lyrics*

Wear-ing a rain-coat that has four sleeves gets us through all kinds of weath-er.

Chorus:

She will al-ways be the on-ly thing that comes be-tween me and the aw-ful sting

w/dist.
f

*Double tracked at this point (next 6 bars).
**Secondary vocal (cue-size notes) tacet first time.

My Beloved Monster - 3 - 1
PG9662

© 1996 ALMO MUSIC CORP. and SEXY GRANDPA MUSIC (ASCAP)
All Rights Administered by ALMO MUSIC CORP. on behalf of SEXY GRANDPA MUSIC for the World
All Rights Reserved

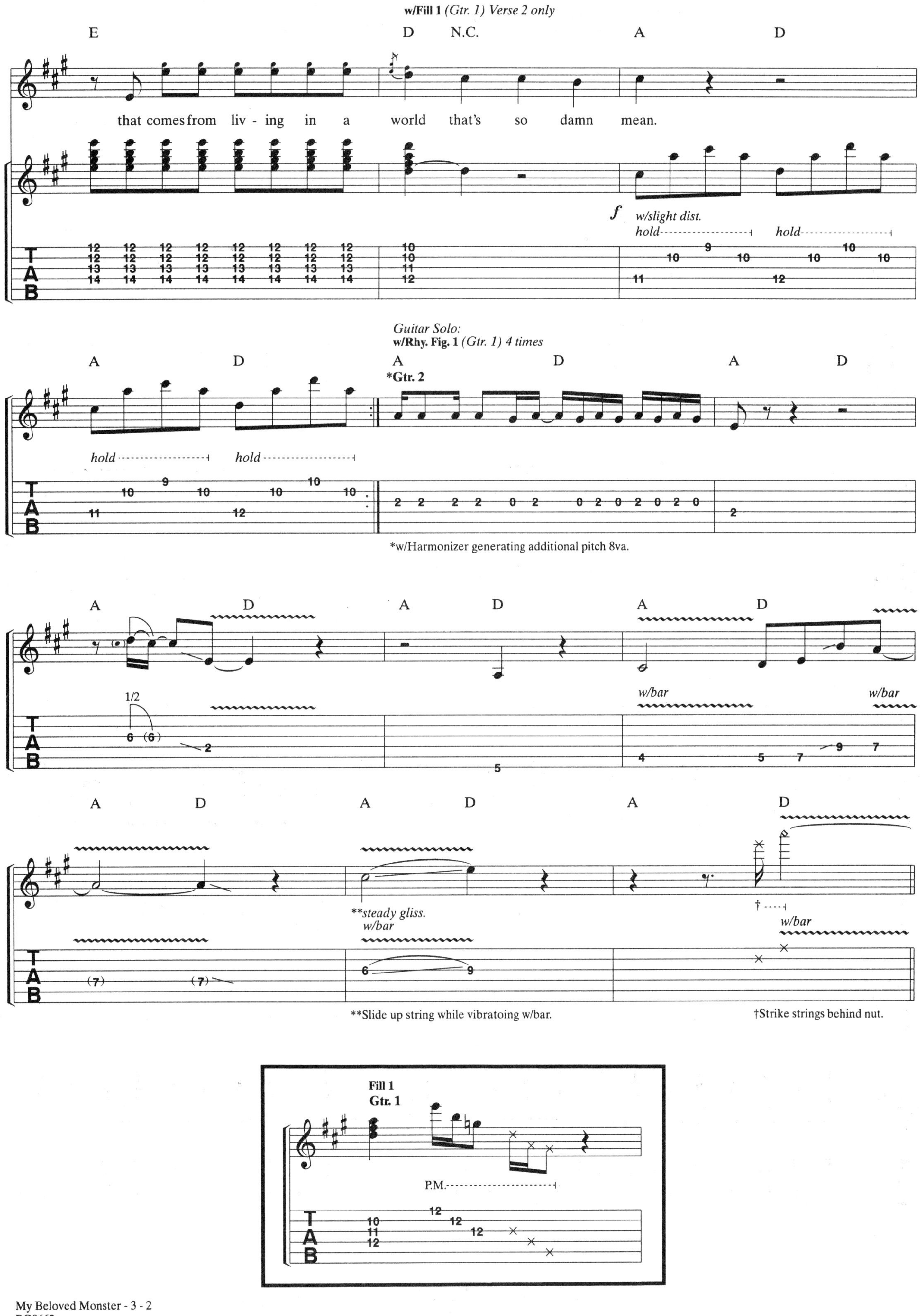
w/Fill 1 (Gtr. 1) Verse 2 only
E
D N.C.
A
D
that comes from liv - ing in a world that's so damn mean.
w/slight dist.
hold
Guitar Solo:
w/Rhy. Fig. 1 (Gtr. 1) 4 times
*Gtr. 2
*w/Harmonizer generating additional pitch 8va.
w/bar
**steady gliss.
**Slide up string while vibratoing w/bar.
†Strike strings behind nut.
Fill 1
Gtr. 1
P.M.

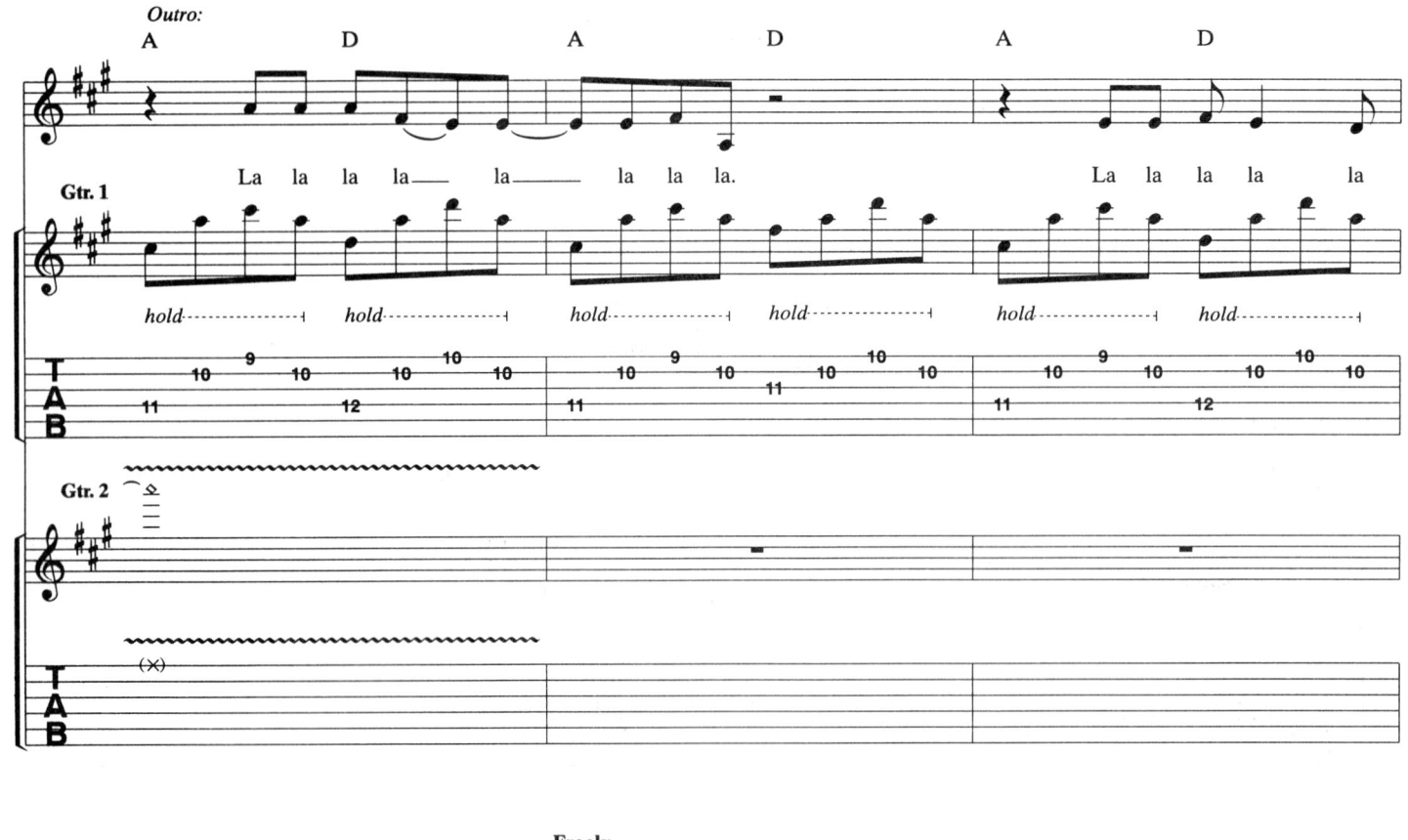

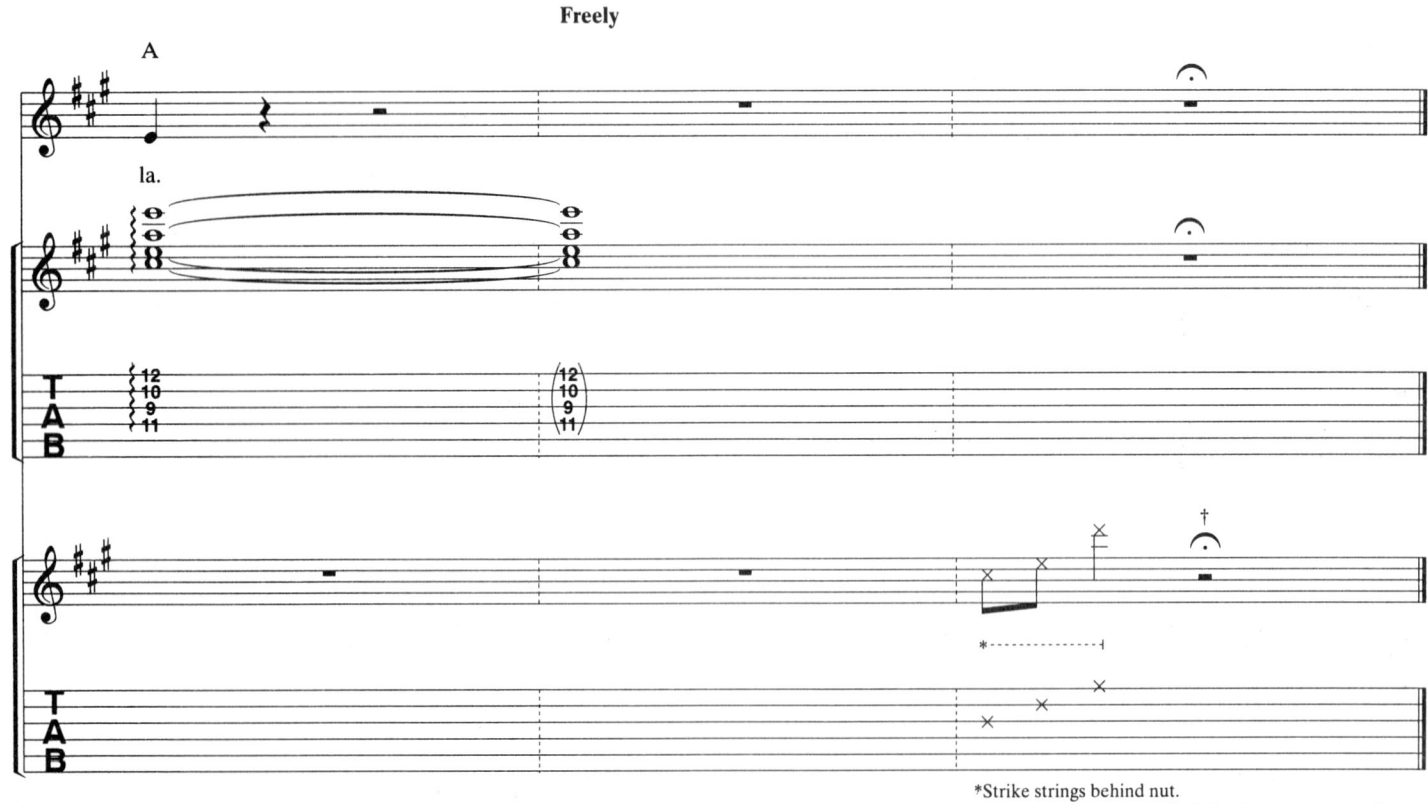

Verse 2:
My beloved monster is tough,
If she wants she will disrobe you.
But if you lay her down for a kiss,
Her little heart, it could explode.
(To Chorus:)

guest list

Words and Music by
E

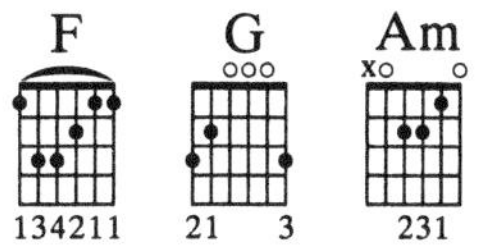

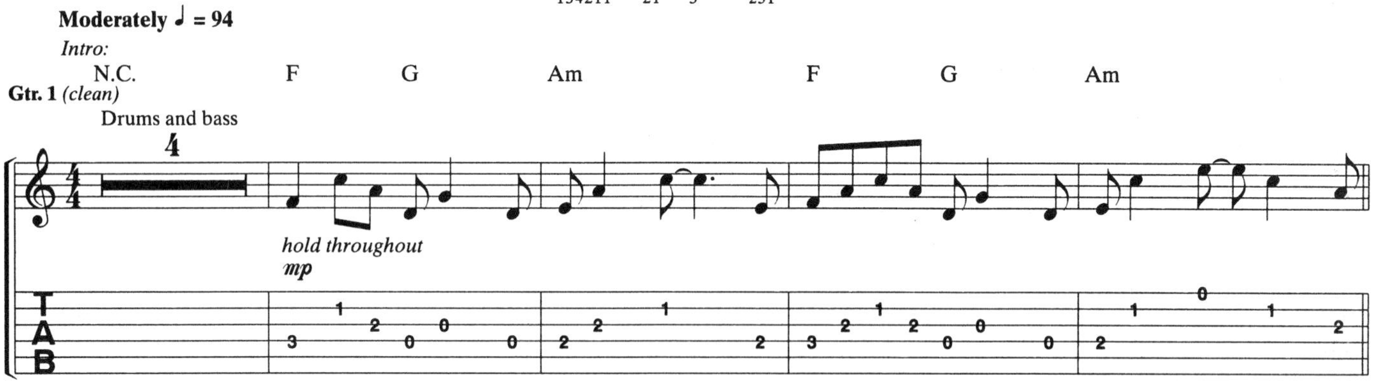

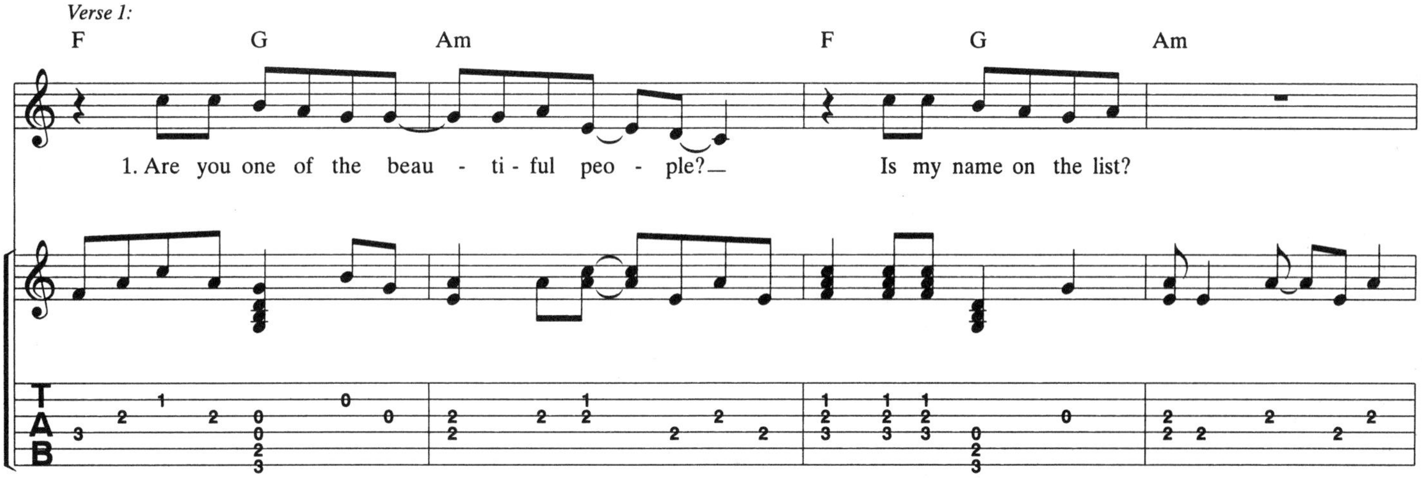

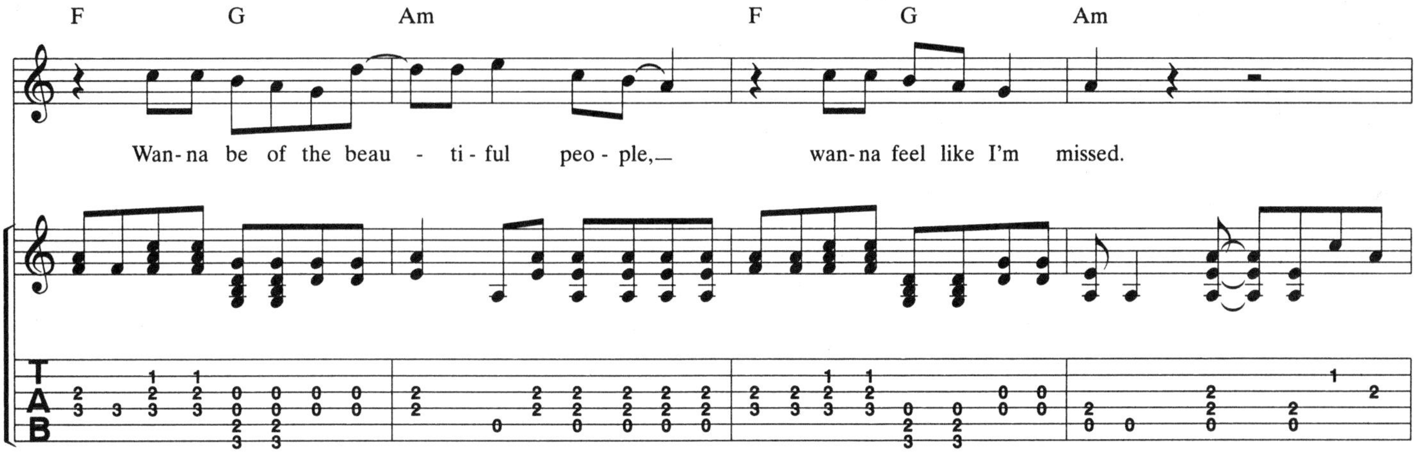

Verses 2 & 3:

2. Hey you,   with the walk-ie-talk-ie,   I know my clothes are not right.
3. *See additional lyrics*

I wish I had my own walk-ie-talk-ie___ that reached to God ev-'ry night.

Gtr. 1 Fill 1

w/slight dist.
mf

Gtr. 2 Fill 1A

w/slight dist.
mf

Guest List - 5 - 2
PG9662

Chorus:

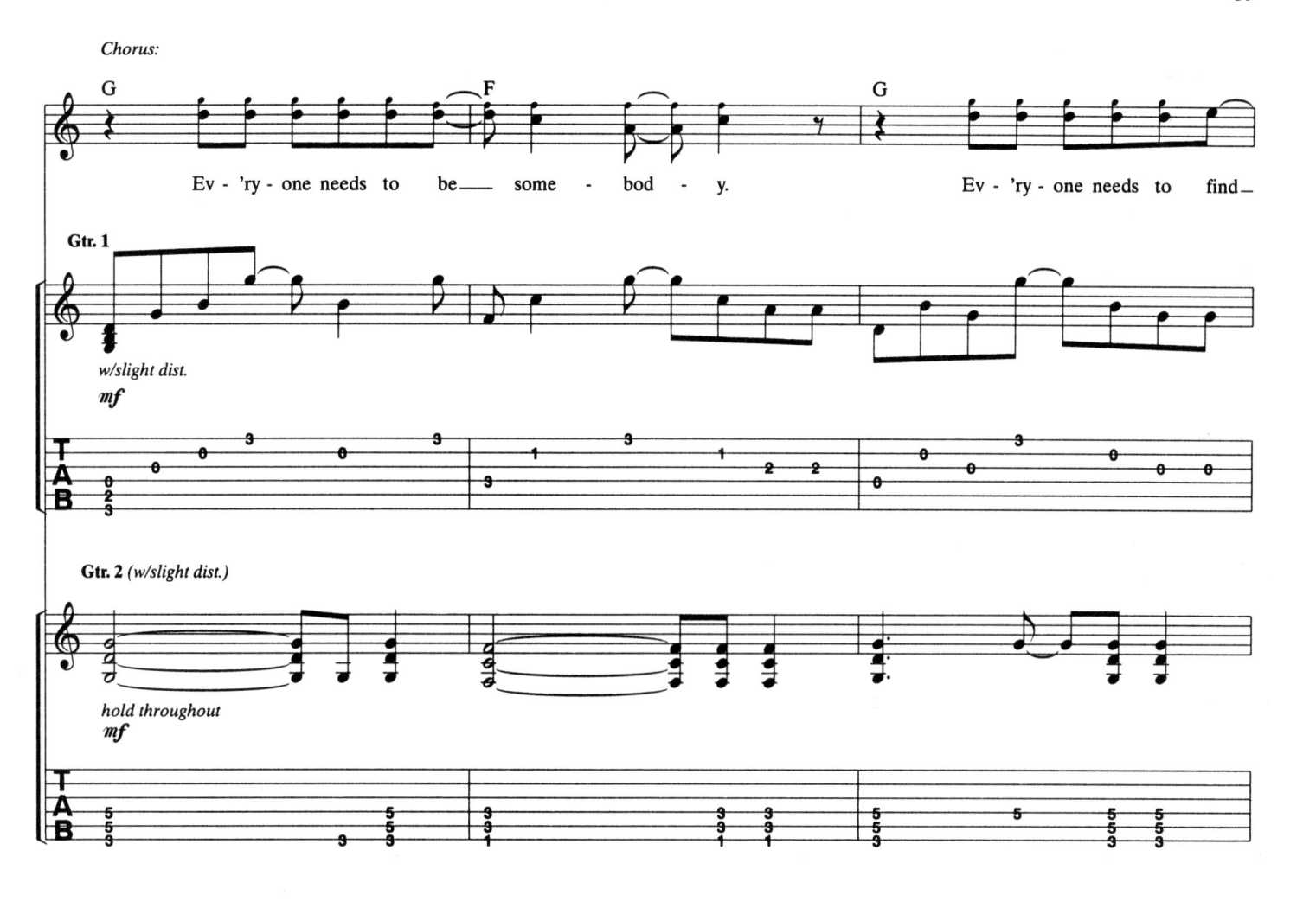

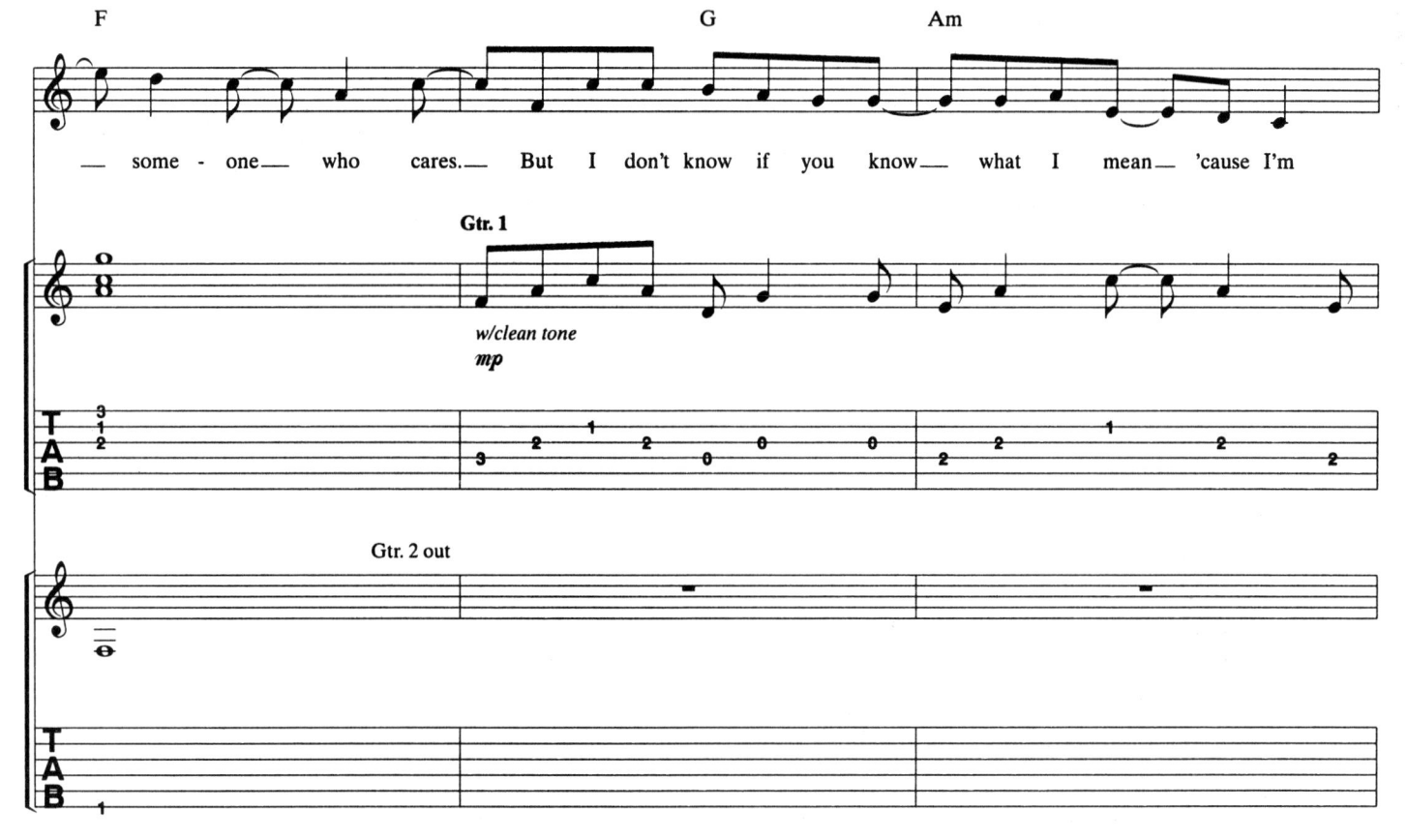

Ev - 'ry - one needs to be— some - bod - y. Ev - 'ry - one needs to find— some - one— who cares.— But I don't know if you know— what I mean— 'cause I'm

Gtr. 1 *w/slight dist.* *mf*

Gtr. 2 *(w/slight dist.)* hold throughout *mf*

Gtr. 1 *w/clean tone* *mp*

Gtr. 2 out

Guest List - 5 - 3
PG9662

To Coda
Harmonica Solo:
F G Am F G
Gtr. 1
never on your list.
Gtr. 2
Cont. in slashes
w/clean tone
mp
Am F G Am
F G Am F G Am
D.S. al Coda
Coda
F G Am F G
I'm never on your list.
I'm never on your

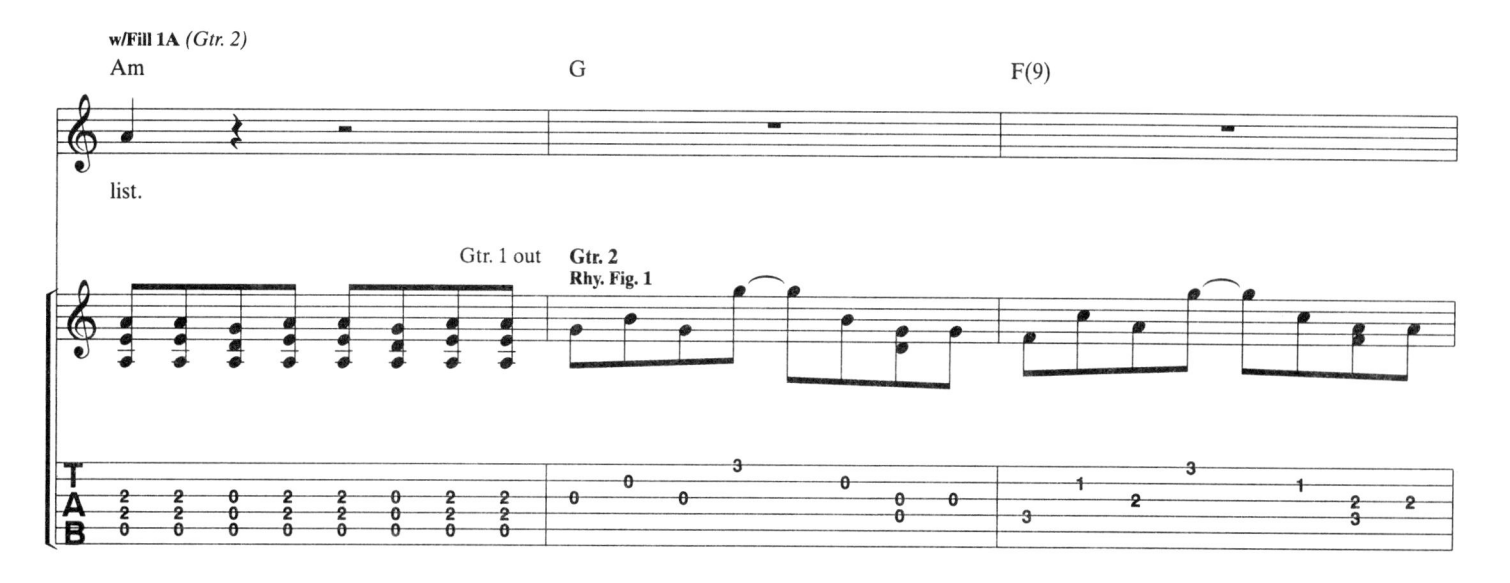

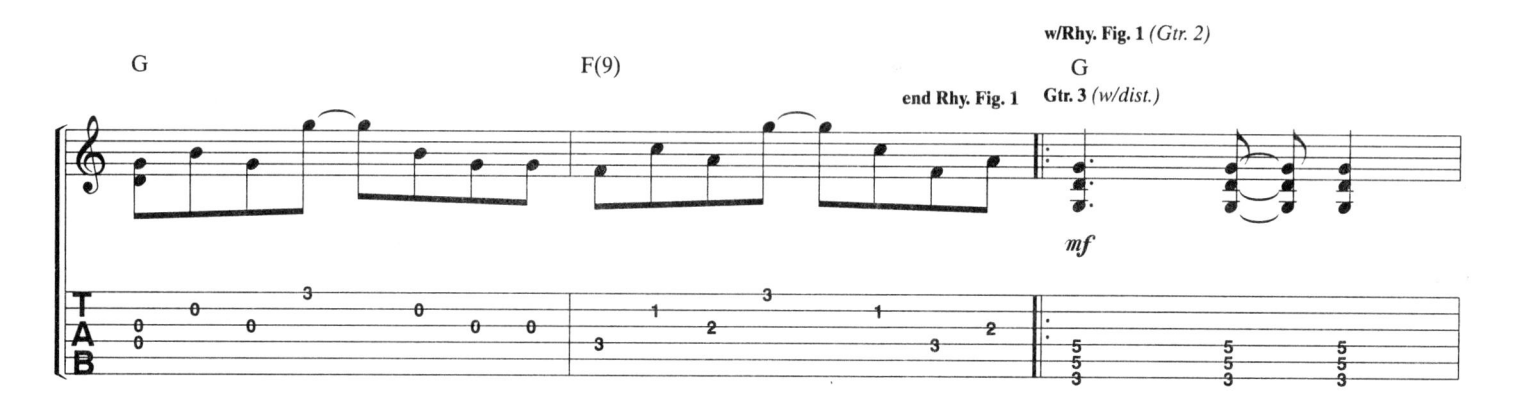

Verse 3:
Are you one of the beautiful people?
Am I on the wrong track?
Sometimes it feels like I'm made of eggshell,
And it feels like I'm gonna crack.
(To Chorus:)

flower

Words and Music by
E and JIM JACOBSEN

Moderately slow ♩ = 70

1. Turn the ugly light off, God, wanna feel the night.
2.3. See additional lyrics

Ev-'ry day it shines down on me; don't you think that I see?

Don't you think that I see what it's all about?

© 1996 ALMO MUSIC CORP. (ASCAP), WB MUSIC CORP. (ASCAP),
CALLIPYGIAN MUSIC (ASCAP) and SEXY GRANDPA MUSIC (ASCAP)
All Rights on behalf of CALLIPYGIAN MUSIC Administered by WB MUSIC CORP.
All Rights Reserved

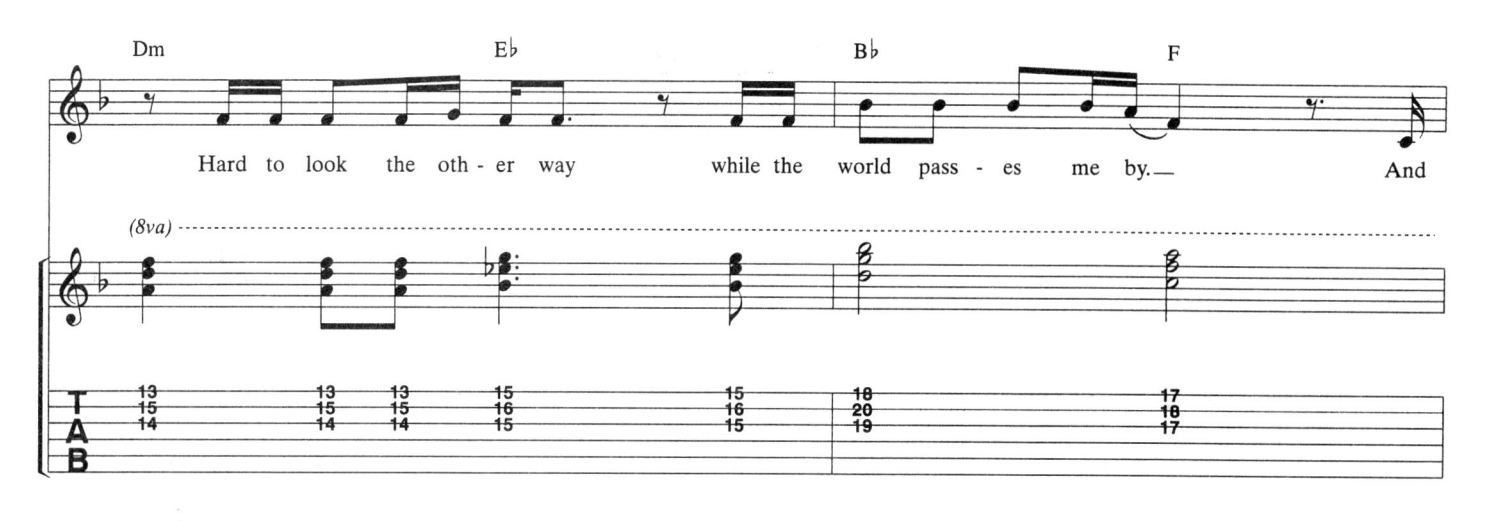

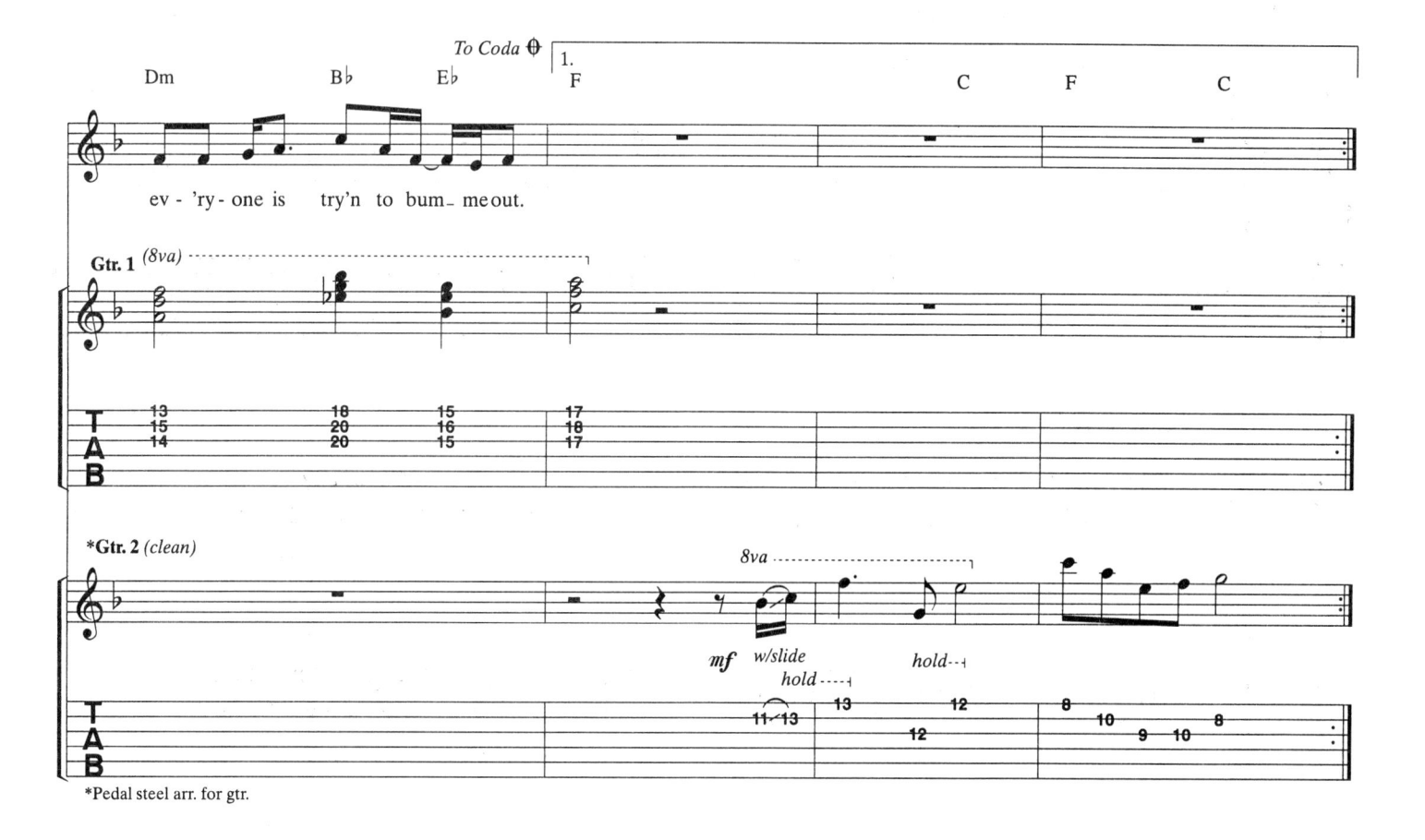

Lyrics:

Hard to look the other way while the world passes me by. And ev-'ry-one is try'n to bum me out.

*Pedal steel arr. for gtr.

Bridge: When I came in-to this world, they slapped

Flower - 4 - 2

44

Verse 2:
It's a pretty big world, God, and I am awful small.
Everyday they rain down on me, flower in a hailstorm.
Flower in a hailstorm, I'm living for the drought.
I could throw it back at them, but then I play their game.
Everyone is trying to bum me out.

Verse 3:
Turn the ugly light off, God, don't wanna see my face.
Every day it will betray me; don't you think that I know?
Don't you think that I know what they're talking about?
If they step on me tonight, they're gonna pay someday.
Everyone is trying to bum me out.

mental

Words and Music by
E

Moderately fast ♩ = 120

Intro: N.C.
Bass & drums

Verse 1: Dm ... Am
1. It's like I dressed up in my ma-ma's cloth-ing.

Gtr. 1 *(clean)*
Rhy. Fig. 1
mp

Dm ... Am ... Gm7 ... A
It's like I'm talk-ing to a voice that does-n't ex - ist.

end Rhy. Fig. 1
hold------
hold------

Verses 2 & 5:
w/Rhy. Fig. 1 *(Gtr. 1)*
w/Fill 1 *(Gtr. 2) Verse 2 only*

Dm ... Am ... Dm
2. It's like I got a wire— crossed up-stairs. But all I want is just a
5. *See additional lyrics*

Fill 1
Gtr. 2   Gtr. 2 out

Mental - 6 - 1
PG9662

© 1996 ALMO MUSIC CORP. and SEXY GRANDPA MUSIC (ASCAP)
All Rights Administered by ALMO MUSIC CORP. on behalf of SEXY GRANDPA MUSIC for the World
All Rights Reserved

Am
Gm7
A
*Gtr. 2
mp
mf
lit - tle truth__ and that's__ it.__
Gtr. 1
hold
*w/distortion.
Chorus:
Dm
A
Dm
Rhy. Fig. 2A
They say I'm men - tal but I'm just con - fused._
They say I'm men - tal but I've
Rhy. Fig. 2
mf
w/dist.
hold throughout
A
Dm
A
been a - bused._
They say I'm men - tal 'cause I'm not a - mused_ by it all.__
Gm7
To Coda
A
end Rhy. Fig. 2A
N.C.
end Rhy. Fig. 2
Gtr. 1

*w/Rhy. Fig. 1 (Gtr. 1)
Dm Am Dm Am
*w/tremolo effect.
Verse 3:
w/Rhy. Fig. 1 (Gtr. 1)
Dm Am Dm
3. An - oth - er an - chor - man is on the T___ V. He's got that far a - way and
Am Gm7 A
va - cant look___ in his___ eye.___
Gtrs. 1 & 2
Verse 4:
Dm Am Dm
4. I turn the chan - nel but noth - ing is chang - ing. The on - ly truth is that
Am Gm7 A
ev - 'ry - thing___ is a lie.___
mf w/slight dist.

49

Chorus:
w/Rhy. Figs. 2 *(Gtr. 1)* & **2A** *(Gtr. 2)*

They say I'm men-tal but I'm just con-fused.___ They say I'm men-tal but I've been a-bused.___ They say I'm men-tal 'cause I'm not a-mused___ by it all.___

*Octaver generates additional pitch 8vb.

Guitar Solo:
w/Rhy. Fig. 1 *(Gtr. 1) 2 times*

Gtr. 2

D.S. 𝄋 al Coda

Mental - 6 - 4
PG9662

Coda
Am
Gm7
Not at all.
Rhy. Fig. 3
Rhy. Fig. 3A
A
Gm7
A
Not at all.
Not at all.
end Rhy. Fig. 3
end Rhy. Fig. 3A

Verse 5:
There's truth in everything, there's truth in lies.
With all this knowledge, well, I think I'm gonna be wise.
(To Chorus:)

spunky

Words and Music by
E

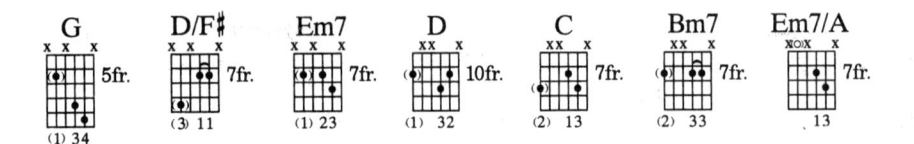

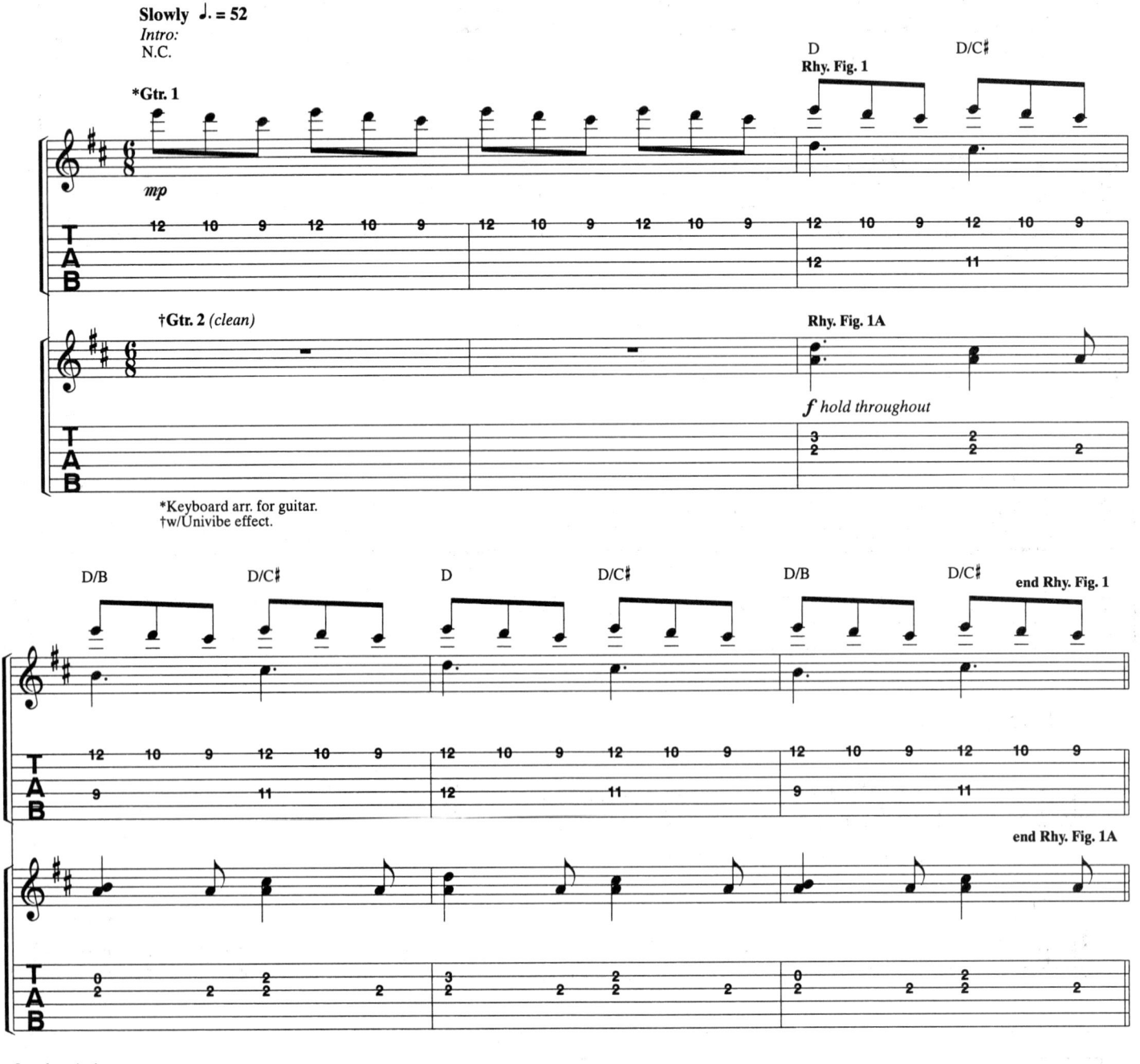

© 1996 ALMO MUSIC CORP. and SEXY GRANDPA MUSIC (ASCAP)
All Rights Administered by ALMO MUSIC CORP. on behalf of SEXY GRANDPA MUSIC for the World
All Rights Reserved

*Gtr. 1 sounds one octave higher. (Octaver generates additional pitch 8va.)

w/Rhy. Fig. 3 (Gtr. 2) simile
D D/C♯ D/B D/C♯ D D/C♯ D/B D/C
cat named Lo-la with a vio-lent past is balled-up a-sleep 'cross her knees. And it's a
Chorus:
w/Rhy. Figs. 1 (Gtr. 1) & 1A (Gtr. 2)
D D/C♯ D/B D/C♯ D D/C♯ D/B D/C♯
free for all, free for all, free for all. It's a free for all, you and me.
D D/C♯ D/B D/C D D/C♯ D/B D/C♯
One day the world will be read-y for you and won-der how they did-n't see.
*Gtr. 3 (clean)
mf
*w/Univibe effect.
Interlude:
G D/F♯ Em7 D C Bm7 Em7/A D
Gtr. 2
Gtr. 1
Gtr. 3

Verse 4:
Spunky knows she can save the world
In her own little way.
Turning in her old uniform
'Cause you know it really didn't pay.
(To Chorus:)

Verse 5:
I'll walk through the world with your name on my tongue
And your picture etched on my screen.

your lucky day in hell

Words and Music by
E and MARK GOLDENBERG

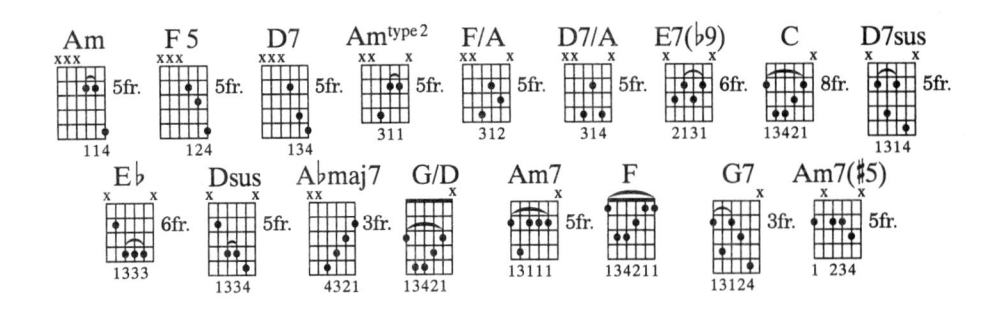

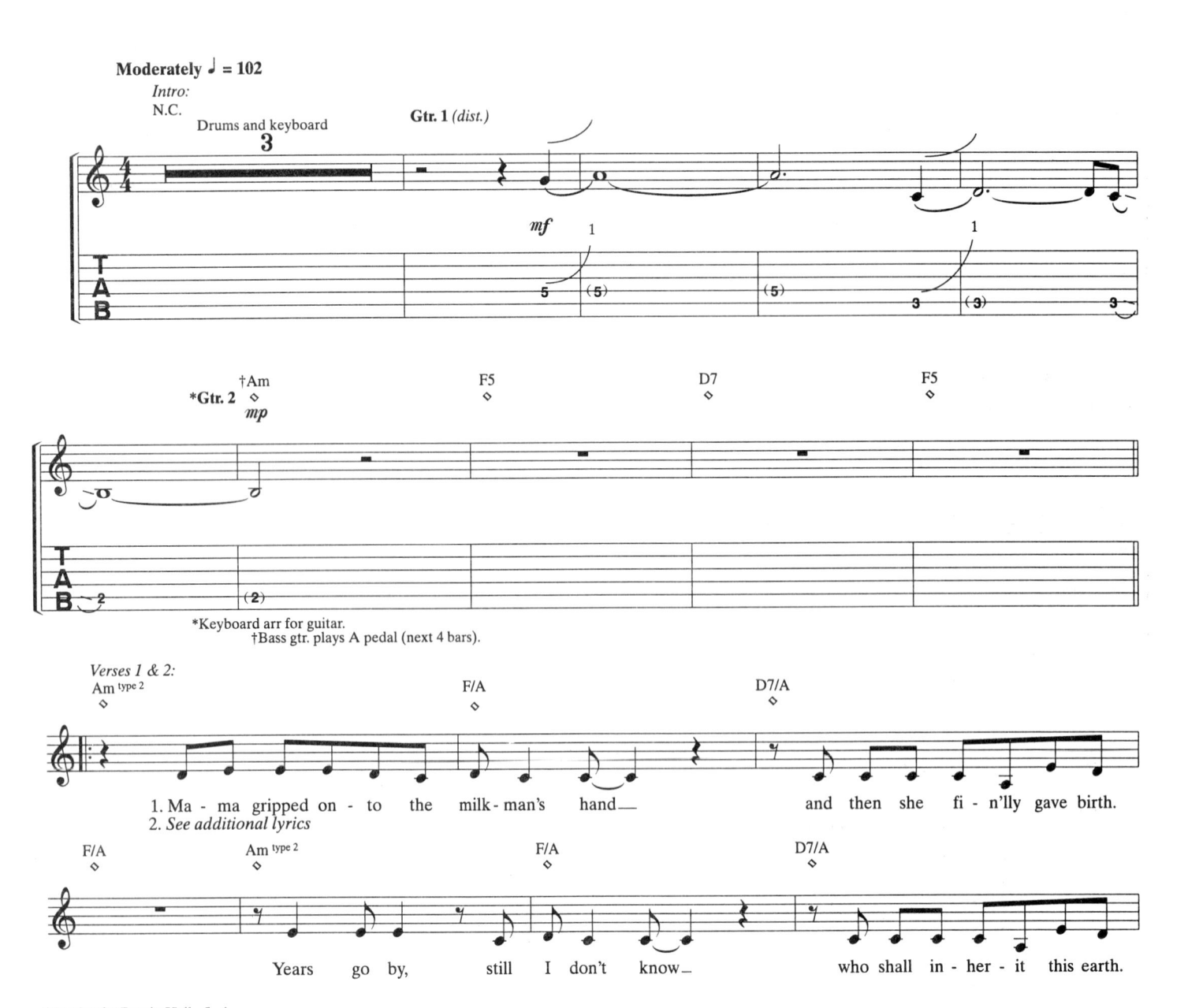

Moderately ♩ = 102

Intro:
N.C.
Drums and keyboard   Gtr. 1 (dist.)

*Keyboard arr for guitar.
†Bass gtr. plays A pedal (next 4 bars).

Verses 1 & 2:

1. Ma-ma gripped on-to the milk-man's hand and then she fi-n'lly gave birth.
2. See additional lyrics

Years go by, still I don't know who shall in-her-it this earth.

Your Lucky Day in Hell - 5 - 1
PG9662

© 1996 ALMO MUSIC CORP. and SEXY GRANDPA MUSIC (ASCAP) and
LONGITUDE MUSIC CO. and FAUX MUSIC (BMI)
All Rights Administered by ALMO MUSIC CORP. on behalf of SEXY GRANDPA MUSIC for the World
All Rights Reserved

w/Fill 1 (Gtr. 1) Verse 2 only
F/A
Am type 2
*F/A
And no one will know my name un - til
Gtr. 1
*Bass gtr. plays F.
*D7/A
E7(♭9)
Chorus:
C
it's on a stone, oh, woah.
This could
Gtr. 3 (clean)
Rhy. Fig. 1
mp w/wah wah
*Bass gtr. plays D.
D7sus
E♭
Dsus
w/Rhy. Fig. 1 (Gtr. 3)
C
be your luck - y day in hell.
Nev - er
end Rhy. Fig. 1
D7sus
E♭
Dsus
know who it might be at your door - bell.
Fill 1
Gtr. 1
hold bend

C
D7sus
E♭
A♭maj7
To Coda
This could be your luck - y day in hell, in hell.
Gtr. 3
Rhy. Fig. 2
hold
1.
2.
Interlude:
Am
F5
end Rhy. Fig. 2
Gtr. 1
Gtr. 3
Gtr. 3 out
hold
D7
F5
Gtr. 2
G
Fa - ther The -
Gtr. 1
grad. dive w/bar

resa, you can't make me in-to you. I nev-er wan-na be like you. Why can't you see it's me? You know it's time to let me go.

Outro Chorus:
in hell. This could be your luck-y day in hell. Nev-er

Verse 2:
Waking up with an ugly face,
Winston Churchill in drag.
Looking for a new maternal embrace,
Another tired old gag.
Am I just a walking bag of chewed up dust and bones?

61

manchild

Words and Music by
E and JILL SOBULE

Slowly ♩. = 66

Intro:
N.C.

Gtr. 1 (clean)
Rhy. Fig. 1
E   A   end Rhy. Fig. 1
mp
hold   hold

Verses 1 & 2:
w/Rhy. Fig. 1 (Gtr. 1) 2 times
E   A
1. And ev-'ry time you crave for me, I'm here.
2. See additional lyrics

E   A
And an-y-thing you hun-ger for, I'll share. And

F#m   B/F#
I will be qui-et-ly stand-ing by,   while

Gtr. 1
hold   hold

Manchild - 3 - 1
PG9662

© 1996 ALMO MUSIC CORP. (ASCAP), WARNER-TAMERLANE PUBLISHING CORP. (BMI),
I'LL SHOW YOU PUBLISHING (BMI) and SEXY GRANDPA MUSIC (ASCAP)
All Rights on behalf of I'LL SHOW YOU PUBLISHING Administered by WARNER-TAMERLANE PUBLISHING CORP.
All Rights Reserved

F♯m
B/F♯
slow - ly I am dy - ing in - side.
hold
hold
Chorus:
E B/D♯ C♯m E/G♯ D A E B/D♯ C♯m E/G♯
Hold me in your arms and let me be the
hold
hold
hold
hold
hold
hold
D B D A B
one who can feel like I am a child in love.
hold
hold
hold
hold
hold
Bridge:
D A D
Whis - per now and tell me how you'll watch me, and tell me some -
hold
hold
hold
T
A
B

Verse 2:
Every time I talk to you, you're down.
And every time you need a laugh, I'm around.
And when you forget I'm here, I'm not.
It isn't really me that you forgot.
(To Chorus:)

GUITAR TAB GLOSSARY **

TABLATURE EXPLANATION

READING TABLATURE: Tablature illustrates the six strings of the guitar. Notes and chords are indicated by the placement of fret numbers on a given string(s).

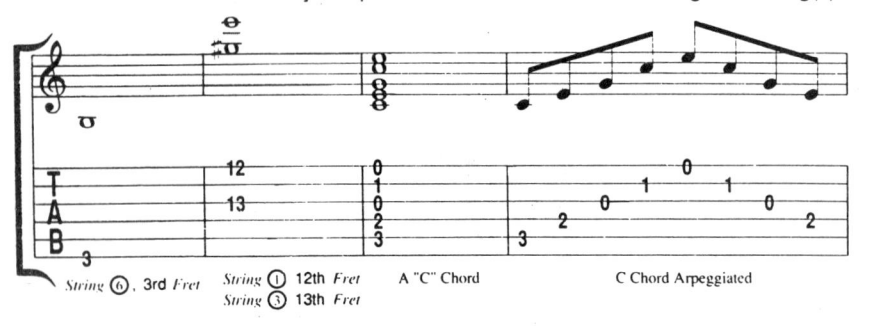

String ⑥, 3rd Fret
String ①, 12th Fret
String ③, 13th Fret
A "C" Chord
C Chord Arpeggiated

BENDING NOTES

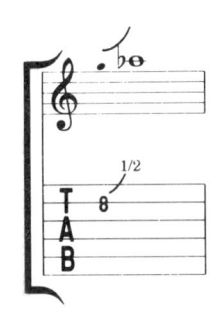

HALF STEP: Play the note and bend string one half step.*

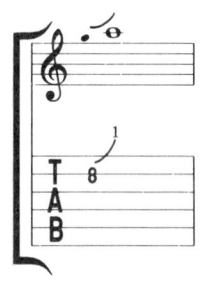

WHOLE STEP: Play the note and bend string one whole step.

PREBEND AND RELEASE: Bend the string, play it, then release to the original note.

RHYTHM SLASHES

STRUM INDICATIONS: Strum with indicated rhythm. The chord voicings are found on the first page of the transcription underneath the song title.

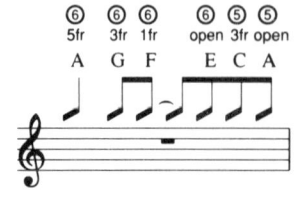

INDICATING SINGLE NOTES USING RHYTHM SLASHES: Very often single notes are incorporated into a rhythm part. The note name is indicated above the rhythm slash with a fret number and a string indication.

*A half step is the smallest interval in Western music; it is equal to one fret. A whole step equals two frets.

**By Kenn Chipkin and Aaron Stang

ARTICULATIONS

HAMMER ON: Play lower note, then "hammer on" to higher note with another finger. Only the first note is attacked.

PULL OFF: Play higher note, then "pull off" to lower note with another finger. Only the first note is attacked.

LEGATO SLIDE: Play note and slide to the following note. (Only first note is attacked).

PALM MUTE: The note or notes are muted by the palm of the pick hand by lightly touching the string(s) near the bridge.

ACCENT: Notes or chords are to be played with added emphasis.

DOWN STROKES AND UPSTROKES: Notes or chords are to be played with either a downstroke (⊓) or upstroke (∨) of the pick.

© 1990 Beam Me Up Music
c/o CPP/Belwin, Inc. Miami, Florida 33014
International Copyright Secured   Made in U.S.A.   All Rights Reserved